TAKING BACK ADVENT

MOVING FROM THE MUNDANE TO THE MIRACULOUS

NANCY GOLDEN

Published by
Golden Cross Ranch LLC

Cover Photo by geralt / pixabay.com

Cover Design by Golden Cross Ranch LLC

In Loving Memory of my Mother
Leah Venetucci
"The apple doesn't fall far from the tree"

INTRODUCTION

The beginning of Advent marks the first day of the Christian liturgical calendar and is a time of anticipation and preparation for the birth of our Lord Jesus Christ. We often allow the hectic pace of the Christmas season to overtake us. The days before Christmas seem to fly by as parties, shopping, tree-lighting, family outings, concerts, and church activities fill our calendars and vie for our attention.

While the hustle and bustle can be overwhelming, I propose that we can take back Advent without sacrificing the activities that bring us joy during this busy season. We do this by starting each day with a brief devotional that gives us an opportunity to move away from the mundane and set our focus on the miracle of Christmas:

> *She will give birth to a son, and you are to give him the name Jesus, because he will save his people from their sins.*
> *Matthew 1:21*

While the start of Advent fluctuates each year and traditionally begins on the fourth Sunday before Christmas, this daily devotional starts as an entry point into the Advent season on December 1st. At the end of each devotional is a section called Today's Activity, and there you will find suggestions on how to implement what you have been reading about. Nothing complicated, just small ways to help you move from the mundane to the miraculous during the course of your day. I pray this devotional blesses you and enables you to take back Advent as you move through the Christmas season!

DAY ONE

Today is the first day of Advent, a sacred and special time of year. During Advent we prepare our hearts for the coming of our Lord Jesus Christ. The celebration of Advent includes looking back and celebrating the birth of Jesus in a stable in Bethlehem, while also looking forward with anticipation to his Second Coming – realizing the promises and prophecies of the Bible. When Jesus first came to the world, it was in humble beginnings as a suffering servant, fulfilling the prophecies of Isaiah 53. In his Second Coming, Jesus will arrive as the conquering King with the armies of heaven at his side (Revelation 19:11-16). Advent is a time of remembrance and anticipation for both.

As we begin the Advent season, let us ponder on the mystery of it all. How the King of kings and Lord of lords loved us so much that he left the heavenly realms to live among us. The fact that he was willing to do so should take our breath away in wonderment and awe. Knowing with certainty that he will come again is cause to rejoice. Let us wait with hopeful anticipation. Come, Lord Jesus! Come!

TODAY'S ACTIVITY: Take some time today and read the Christmas story in Luke 1-2. Go outside this evening and look up into the night sky. Imagine you can see the star of Bethlehem. As you start preparing your heart for the birth of our Savior, ask God to help you renew your feelings of joy and anticipation - so that you can begin to take your Advent experience from the mundane to the miraculous!

DAY TWO

As we journey into the Advent season, let us reflect on why Jesus came down from heaven to live and move among us. Matthew 1:21 says, "She will give birth to a son, and you are to give him the name Yeshua, because he will save his people from their sins." Yeshua is Hebrew for "the Lord shall save," and can be interpreted to refer to the atoning work of Jesus at the cross. He came here to save us! Iesous is the Greek transliteration of the Hebrew name Yeshua, and its English spelling is "Jesus," the name we find in our English Bibles. As his name reflects, the birth of Jesus is part of God's plan to save us from our sins, so that we may have eternal life with Him.

God gave Jesus his name and, by doing so, announced to the world that He had provided a Savior for us, a way out of the predicament that we all find ourselves in. Romans 6:23 tells us, "For the wages of sin is death, but the gift of God is eternal life in Christ Jesus our Lord."

God gave us the greatest gift of all on Christmas morning, in the humblest of surroundings: a manger. He sent His Son Jesus into the world to save us from the consequences of our sin, and Jesus willingly went. What kind of love drives that? What kind of love leaves the glories of heaven to be born in a stable and to walk upon a broken world and call it his home? Only an incomprehensible, unconditional, passionate love could do that. That was the love that was born on Christmas day!

Today's Activity: Think of all of the gifts you have received in the past. Many of them came to you in beautifully wrapped packages, or with some type of fanfare. Now imagine being handed a brown cardboard box. Don't let its plain appearance fool you. You can't tell a gift by its wrapping. Open it slowly and peer inside. See in your mind's eye a baby, born in a lowly manger, God's gift of eternal life to you, in Christ Jesus. The packaging isn't auspicious, but the contents are precious beyond measure!

DAY THREE

Love was born on Christmas day, and Jesus demonstrated that love all throughout his earthly ministry. Hebrews 4:15 tells us, "For we do not have a high priest who is unable to empathize with our weaknesses, but we have one who has been tempted in every way, just as we are—yet he did not sin." While Jesus coming to live among us was part of God's plan for the redemption of our sins, his presence also accomplished many other purposes. Our Lord is not distant from us, he is Immanuel, "God with us." As a result, he has experienced the entire spectrum of human emotions. Jesus walked in the chaotic swirl of humanity and saw the people he loved filled with gladness and overcome with sorrow. Although God is his father, he also had earthly parents and brothers and sisters and experienced growing up in a family with all of the joys and challenges that entails. He felt loneliness. He experienced anger at injustice, and he knows what it feels like to be rejected, betrayed, and persecuted.

We can take great comfort in the fact that Jesus understands us, for he was one of us. In a lowly stable, he was born accessible to us, and he remains accessible today. The love that carried him to the cross is everlasting, and when we are feeling over-whelmed and we feel like no one understands – he does. During this Advent season we can be grateful in knowing that "God with us" is also "God who understands us."

TODAY'S ACTIVITY: How wonderful it is that we can bring all of our burdens to Jesus and ask him to help us! Meditate on Philip-pians 4:6-7 and apply it in your life today. Make some time to talk to Jesus and let him know what is on your mind. Slowly read Romans 8:35-39 and let the beauty of Paul's words sink in. Be still and feel God's loving presence envelope you and know with supreme confidence that nothing can separate you from His love.

DAY FOUR

While Advent is a season of joy as we anticipate our Savior's coming, the Christmas season can also be a difficult time for those who are grieving a loved one that has gone on to be with our Lord. You may have heard someone ask, "What is the shortest verse in the Bible?" and the answer that is typically provided, John 11:35, "Jesus wept." While this is true in many English versions of the Bible, the significance of that verse goes far beyond its reputation about being brief. "Jesus wept" also lovingly demonstrates what we talked about in yesterday's devotional – that "God with us" is also "God who understands us."

The circumstances that resulted in this verse is one that we all struggle with at some time in our lives – the death of someone dear to us. Jesus loved Lazarus (John 11:5) but knew that saying goodbye to his friend did not mean eternal separation (in fact, he knew that he would be raising Lazarus from the dead, so the separation would be ending that very day), yet he still wept because his friend had exited this world and those who loved him were filled with grief at his death. John 11:33 tells us, "When Jesus saw her (Mary, Lazarus' sister) weeping, and the Jews who had come with her also weeping, he was deeply moved in his spirit and greatly troubled." Jesus understood the separation of loved ones, even if temporary from the eternal perspective of heaven, is cause for great sorrow in the human heart.

If you are grieving a loved one this Advent season, you can be confident that Jesus has great compassion for you and for what you are feeling. One of the most moving passages of Scripture is Revelation 21:4, "He will wipe away every tear from their eyes, and death shall be no more, neither shall there be mourning, nor crying, nor pain anymore, for the former things have passed away." We have that promise for the future, but we also have the reality of God's love for us now. Jesus empathizes with you in your mourning, and he weeps because you weep. If you are experiencing this difficult season during Advent, I pray that the God of all comfort comforts you, and that you can find peace knowing that our Savior loves you and weeps with you.

Today's Activity: If you are grieving the loss of someone you love, try to reach out to those around you. It's tempting to shut the world away, but it's important to allow others to help you as you walk this difficult journey. You may want to consider attending a grief support group such as Grief Share, which is offered by many churches. You can find more information at griefshare.org.

If you know someone who is grieving, be intentional about staying connected with them. Mail them a "thinking of you" card, text them an encouraging message, or invite them to dinner. Often many people reach out during the initial period of loss, but grieving can continue for months or even years afterwards, and continuing to show you care can provide healing comfort to a broken heart.

DAY FIVE

By now, you have probably noticed that the stores are decorated and filled with Christmas inventory. Christmas music fills the air. Everywhere we go, we are bombarded with Christmas advertisements, which have the ultimate goal of promoting sales. The peace of Advent feels assaulted with worldly entrapments as we go about our days, and "Happy Holidays" is heard over "Merry Christmas" as the greeting of choice, often dictated by store upper management.

While I know many Christians who struggle with the commercialization of Christmas, for me, Philippians 1:18 comes to mind. Paul says, "The important thing is that in every way, whether from false motives or true, Christ is preached. And because of this I rejoice." While some would use Christmas solely as a means to profit, even they can't deny the reason for the season: no Christ...no Christmas. As we move through this beautiful time of reflection, it is good to remember God's ultimate purposes. Jesus came to earth to save all of us, and Christmas opens doors to talk about our Savior naturally.

Christmas is a great time to share about why you are excited to celebrate the birth of Christ. 1 Peter 3:15 says, "But in your hearts revere Christ as Lord. Always be prepared to give an answer to everyone who asks you to give the reason for the hope that you have. But do this with gentleness and respect." So rather than getting upset over a greeting that a retail employee has no choice but to utter, or about the lack of Christ in Christmas in some venues, let us show the reason for the season: by being a loving example to those around us.

Advent is a time of hopeful expectation, but we should not be idle while we wait. Kingdom work is all around us. Be kind to the retail workers that are finding themselves exhausted as they work long hours through the holiday season. Feed the hungry, minister to the brokenhearted, tip your waiter or waitress extra generously. "Thank you for your work – God bless you!" is a phrase you can use with a warm smile throughout your day to those who serve you. A smile and a kind greeting go a long way to make someone's hectic day a little bit brighter. Let's be a light for Christ even as we await his coming.

Today's Activity: Write down three things you can do to love others, and act upon them. You can offer construction workers cold bottled water and thank them for their work. You can take the time to engage your checker in conversation - ask them how they are doing. If you see parents out with their children, you can tell them what a beautiful family they have. You can hold a door open for someone and wish them a good day. You can offer to pray for someone who looks distressed in the doctor's office waiting room.

Look around and be intentional about creating opportunities to show Christ to others - the possibilities are endless!

DAY SIX

As we await our Lord Jesus with excitement and anticipation, we are filled with hope. What a joy it is to be a Christ-follower! As we travel through life as temporary inhabitants of this world, we know where our true citizenship lies. "Biblical hope" is much different from how we usually use the word "hope" in our day-to-day conversations. Have you ever said, "I hope to get a raise?" or "I hope we can go to the beach on vacation next year?" or "I hope they have that shirt in my size?" All of those statements imply uncertainty – there is no guarantee that what we are hoping for will come to fruition.

Biblical hope is not like that. It is not based on circumstances, but rather, on the promises and character of God. This hope is not a wishful, uncertain desire, but a confident certainty and a blessed assurance for those who follow Christ. Paul writes in Romans 5:3-4, "And not only this, but we also exult in our tribulations, knowing that tribulation brings about perseverance; and perseverance, proven character; and proven character, hope;"

Paul uses the Greek word ἐλπίς [transliterated as *elpis*] in this verse. It is the hope we have in Jesus as our Risen Lord who has overcome death. While we travel through the difficulties of a broken world, we are joyful and have a confident expectation of eternal salvation. So as we anticipate the coming of our Lord this Advent season, we also look back to the Resurrection and are filled with joy at the hope we have in him.

Christmas time is a time of family gatherings, and of Christmas parties with friends. It is also the perfect time to share the hope you have with others, so that they too can have the blessed assurance you have.

Blessed Assurance

Blessed assurance, Jesus is mine!
    Oh, what a foretaste of glory divine!
    Heir of salvation, purchase of God,
    Born of His Spirit, washed in His blood.
    Refrain:
    This is my story, this is my song,
    Praising my Savior all the day long;
    This is my story, this is my song,
    Praising my Savior all the day long.

Perfect submission, perfect delight,
    Visions of rapture now burst on my sight;
    Angels, descending, bring from above
    Echoes of mercy, whispers of love.

Perfect submission, all is at rest,
    I in my Savior am happy and blest,
    Watching and waiting, looking above,
    Filled with His goodness, lost in His love.

— Francis J. Crosby

Today's Activity: Can you think of someone within your sphere of influence with whom you can share the hope you have? Be sensitive to the leading of the Holy Spirit and be prepared for spiritual conversations. One of my favorite conversation starters is to say "Christmas is my second favorite holiday of the year," which inevitably leads to the question, "Well, what's your first?" What a great opportunity to explain the hope we have in the Resurrection on Easter Sunday!"

DAY SEVEN

As we are getting closer to Christmas during this Advent season, it is easy to find ourselves overwhelmed with busyness. The pressures of making preparations for family gatherings, Christmas shopping, church activities, and attending Christmas functions can make the days pass in a blur. You may also find your mailbox filled daily with solicitations for donations to various worthy causes. It can be enough to make you to want to pack your bags and escape the holiday frenzy! That is where the example of our Lord Jesus comes in. Luke 5:16 tells us, "But Jesus often withdrew to lonely places and prayed."

All through Scripture, Jesus takes time away from people to spend time with his Father. He understood how important it is to pray for and with others, but he also understood the importance of being alone with God. He often leaves the crowds he is preaching to, and goes up the mountainside so that he can pray alone. He sometimes goes to a garden in the quiet of the evening for prayer.

Jesus ministered to many during his earthly ministry, but he did so according to his Father's will, and he constantly spent time with God. What a great example for us during this Advent season! You are not called to every Christmas activity or event, and you don't have to help everywhere. Quiet your heart and see where God is leading. Don't forget to spend time with Him. As we discussed in a previous devotional, Jesus had multiple purposes for his presence on earth. His greatest purpose is found in Matthew 1:21, *to save us from our sins*, but he is also an example for us in living a life pleasing to God.

Seek God's will in all that you do, and spend time with Him. Psalm 46:10 reads, "Be still, and know that I am God." Perhaps you need to take a pause from the whirlwind of activities around you and let your Lord minister to your soul, as you await his coming.

TODAY'S ACTIVITY: Take some time out of your day today to be still. Make a cup of coffee or tea, seek out your favorite place to relax, and put on some worship music or read your Bible. Put aside the stresses of the day. Don't think about anything except that you are a son or daughter of the one true King. The Creator of the universe loves you and knows you by name. Spend some time with your Heavenly Father and let His healing presence soothe your spirit and touch your soul with His peace.

DAY EIGHT

Today, as we continue on our Advent journey, let us take a moment and reflect on John 3:16, "For God so loved the world that he gave his one and only Son, that whoever believes in him shall not perish but have eternal life." The first half of this verse tells us that "God so loved the WORLD," - not one group of people or one country or race – He loves everyone! Each person is precious to Him and He wants every person to be reconciled to Him.

The second part of the verse tells us how reconciliation happens: "God gave His one and only Son." God in His infinite love for us sent His Son into the world on Christmas morning so that Jesus could do his atoning work at the cross on our behalf. How do we receive the redemption that God provides for us, through His Son?

The last part of the verse holds the answer: "whoever believes in him shall not perish but have eternal life." What an incredible gift God offers us and all we have to do is accept it! As we move through the Christmas season and talk about the birth of Christ, let us remember John 3:16. Jesus is God's gift of love to the world, and His love is for all people.

TODAY'S ACTIVITY: God's gift is for ALL people! Is there someone in your neighborhood, or perhaps a co-worker, who doesn't know Christ? The first step in sharing your faith is to begin building a relationship with them. As trust is built, the Holy Spirit will provide opportunities for spiritual conversations - but you have to START! Today - be intentional. Greet a neighbor or a co-worker and initiate a conversation that focuses on them. Invite them to go with you to your church's Christmas Eve service. The best Christmas gift you can give them is to introduce them to Christ!

DAY NINE

Advent is a season that inspires us to love others. 1 John 4:9-11 says, "This is how God showed his love among us: He sent his one and only Son into the world that we might live through him. This is love: not that we loved God, but that he loved us and sent his Son as an atoning sacrifice for our sins. Dear friends, since God so loved us, we also ought to love one another." As we move through Advent, let's remember those words and take them to heart: love one another. Take note of the people around you. Christmas can be a difficult season for some, and God may have placed people in your life that need to experience His love through you.

Love came down from heaven and was born on Christmas day. As Christ-followers, it is up to us to be a reflection of that love. Ephesians 5:2 tells us, "and walk in the way of love, just as Christ loved us and gave himself up for us as a fragrant offering and sacrifice to God." Jesus tells us in Matthew 22:37-38, "'Love the Lord your God with all your heart and with all your soul and with all your mind.' This is the first and greatest commandment. And the second is like it: 'Love your neighbor as yourself.'"

When we think about how we can love our neighbor, we can

do so in many tangible ways – God might use you as His provision for another through your time and presence, financial assistance, or a gesture of kindness and compassion. Remember that it is a wonderful time to tell the Christmas story and share the greatest gift of all – God's love for us born in a stable, accessible to all.

TODAY'S ACTIVITY: Think of at least one person that you can offer to spend time with. We get so busy with our daily activities that we often forget to stop and give the gift of our time to someone who would deeply appreciate it. Make time for the older people you know - just because life moves at a slower pace doesn't mean they don't need social interaction. In fact, it is more important than ever for their health and longevity.

You can offer tangible assistance: help a single Mom buy Christmas presents for her children. Open your home to an international student or a student unable to go home for the holidays. The possibilities are endless, so take some time to reflect on who God is putting on your heart, and then make a commitment and follow through. You'll be blessed as much as the recipient of your efforts!

DAY TEN

During this season of Advent we are reflecting on God's love for us through the birth of His Son Jesus Christ, as we remember and anticipate his return. How do we define love and how do we express it? We can go to Scripture for the answer. Read the famous "love passage" from 1 Corinthians 13:4-8a,

> Love is patient, love is kind. It does not envy, it does not boast, it is not proud. It does not dishonor others, it is not self-seeking, it is not easily angered, it keeps no record of wrongs. Love does not delight in evil but rejoices with the truth. It always protects, always trusts, always hopes, always perseveres.

> Love never fails.

Let these words sink in. Reflect on each expression of love that is listed, then think about how you can show that kind of love to those around you. You might also reflect on how that love has been shown to you, and thank God for His provision for you through others.

One of the most compelling things about Jesus is that he experienced what it means to be fully human. He understands that sometimes we need people ("Jesus with skin" as I once heard someone say) to be the expression of His love for us. Is that you? Is there someone God has brought into your path today to share His love with? Or have you received that from someone else? You might reach out and encourage them by thanking them for what they have done for you. Jesus came down from heaven to be "God with us" but he also wants us to be God's love to each other. To be "Jesus with skin."

TODAY'S ACTIVITY: How can you be "Jesus with skin" to someone today? Think of someone that has helped you on your journey. Many people spend a lot of time helping others and their efforts are often not recognized. While they are doing it to serve God, it is still nice to hear affirmation from others once in awhile. Reach out to thank them in person, with a phone call, or a handwritten card that they can keep and look at when they are feeling discouraged. You can pop a gift card for a cup of coffee with it as a nice gesture - although the words you express in the card will be treasured much more. "Being Jesus with skin" simply means showing you care.

DAY ELEVEN

This time of year always seems to bring people to mind that we may not have thought about in awhile. A little baby being born in Bethlehem two thousand years ago changed the world in so many ways, and while we journey through Advent and await his coming, it seems we are nicer to each other. We reach out more. God's love is like that. Once you have it, you want to share it with the people around you. Once Jesus resides in your heart, his love overflows.

Jesus is the ultimate gift, sent by God to reconcile us to Him so that we may have eternal life. As we get closer to Christmas, think of the people in your life that you may have a need to reconcile with. Paul writes in Romans 5:8, "But God demonstrates his own love for us in this: While we were still sinners, Christ died for us." God didn't wait for us to be perfect to reach out to us in love (which is a good thing, because we could never attain perfection on our own) and we should follow His example – don't wait to reconcile with anyone that you are at odds with. God forgives us – how can we do any less?

Love came down from heaven and was born on Christmas day. You can follow his example by allowing that love to motivate you to make peace with someone that may have caused you heartache. I know I cause God lots of grief when I don't do the things I should, or I behave badly, but He loves me anyway. Seek out those you need to reconcile with and, like Jesus, love them anyway too. That would be an awesome Christmas gift to give that precious baby born in a manger: the gift of love.

TODAY'S ACTIVITY: Read this blog post: Forgiving Ourselves and Forgiving Others located at:

https://novelwrites.com/2016/04/25/forgiving-ourselves-and-forgiving-others/

Is there someone in your life you need to reach out to, so that healing and restoration can take place? Pray and ask God for His help. Is there someone you know who is struggling with bitterness and needs to hear this message of forgiveness? Help them take a step towards love, so that they can experience peace.

"Be kind and compassionate to one another, forgiving each other, just as in Christ God forgave you." Ephesians 4:32.

DAY TWELVE

As we continue to move through Advent and ponder the love that God has for us, it would be good to get a better understanding of that love. In the English language we use one word to describe many things. We can love our brothers and sisters, we can have a more intimate love for our spouse, we can even love hamburgers, but none of these describe the love that God has for us. When we go back to the original Greek, we see that all of these types of love have a different word assigned to it. Family love or love of an object may fall under Storge στοργή. The brotherly love of friendship is expressed as Philia φιλία, and sexual love as Eros ἔρως. The love of God for man has its own word too. It is called Agape ἀγάπη.

Paulo Coelho beautifully expresses the magnitude of God's Agape love for us: "This was the love that Jesus felt for humanity, and it was so great that it shook the stars and changed the course of man's history."

God's love for us is relentless, incomprehensible, sacrificial, and unconditional. Perfect and without sin, yet willing to die for us - that is the amazing Agape love that God has for us. He is faithful even when we aren't. He doesn't wait for us to clean up our acts – He loves us exactly where we are at, with a fierce love that knows no bounds. The baby born in the manger on Christmas day is His greatest expression of Agape love: God's provision to deliver us from our sins so that we can spend eternity with Him. Agape love was born on Christmas day!

TODAY'S ACTIVITY: Spend some time with God today and allow yourself to soak in His love for you. Play your favorite worship songs and sing your gratitude to the One who loves you beyond comprehension.

DAY THIRTEEN

Advent is a time to reflect on God's love for us, expressed through the coming of His Son Jesus Christ. We live in such tension as Christians in the world today. During a sermon by Pastor Andy McQuitty at Irving Bible Church, he called it living "in-between." We are citizens of heaven longing for Jesus to return as we struggle to make sense of a broken world.

We should always remember that, as the body of Christ, when one rejoices, we also rejoice, and when one suffers, we suffer with them. We should also remember that we are called to bring light to the darkness. Let us pray for one another, encourage each other, and bear one another's burdens. Share the gospel with a world that, like all of us, desperately needs a Savior. It's pretty simple really. Love the Lord your God with all of your heart, soul, mind and strength. Love your neighbor as yourself. Wouldn't it be a wonderful world if we all did that? It will be someday when Christ returns - in the mean time we need to keep our eyes focused on God and reflect His love to those around us.

While it is frustrating to see so much pain and suffering in

the world, we have an advantage - we know how the story ends!
We might have to walk through some very difficult situations in
our lives, but what a blessing to know that we will never walk
through them alone. Do you know someone this Christmas
season without hope in Christ? The greatest act of love you can
do for them is to share with them the hope that you have,
providing the Holy Spirit an opportunity to begin working in
their hearts. It all begins by simply spending time with them
and loving them, and opportunities to share will arise naturally,
especially during this time of year. Don't wait. You never know
what tomorrow may bring.

TODAY'S ACTIVITY: Read 1 Peter 3:15. Make a list of those people
God has put on your heart who are in need of knowing Jesus.
Begin praying specifically for them today and be looking for
Spirit-led opportunities to share the hope you have with them.

DAY FOURTEEN

During this Advent season and throughout the year, how wonderful it is to call upon Christ as Lord and Savior! No matter what is going on in the world - we don't lose heart and we don't lose hope. Jesus is faithful and God has shared with us His redemptive plan for humanity in His Word, that continues to move forward regardless of what is happening around us. Isaiah 43:18-19 says,

> Remember not the former things,
> nor consider the things of old.
> Behold, I am doing a new thing;
> now it springs forth, do you not perceive it?
> I will make a way in the wilderness
> and rivers in the desert.

Through hurricanes, earthquakes, news drama, political disagreements, terrorism, a fast-changing secular society on a moral downslide, and anything else that threatens our peace, God is on His throne. He will make a way and His plans will ultimately prevail. Take hold of what Jesus tells us in John 16:33, and keep this verse close when you are tempted to feel hopeless: "I have told you these things, so that in me you may have peace. In this world you will have trouble. But take heart! I have overcome the world."

We will have trouble but always remember - we are not fighting FOR victory - we are fighting FROM victory. In Revelation 21:5 Jesus tells us, "And he who was seated on the throne said, 'Behold, I am making all things new.' Also he said, 'Write this down, for these words are trustworthy and true.'" Our hope is not an uncertain wish, but rather, a confident assurance that Jesus will return someday and that he will make all things new! Let us reflect on this wondrous truth as we look forward to celebrating his birth and anticipate his return. Come Lord Jesus, Come!

TODAY'S ACTIVITY: Stay off the internet today. Take a day off from social media. Instead, focus on what Paul instructs us to do in Philippians 4:8, "Finally, brothers and sisters, whatever is true, whatever is noble, whatever is right, whatever is pure, whatever is lovely, whatever is admirable—if anything is excellent or praiseworthy—think about such things," and see what a difference it makes in your day!

DAY FIFTEEN

As we journey through Advent, you most likely have been listening to some Christmas music. Perhaps you have participated in singing Christmas carols. Three of the most well known are "Away in a Manger," "Joy to the World," and "O Little Town of Bethlehem." Luke 2:7 tells us, "And she gave birth to her firstborn son and wrapped him in swaddling cloths and laid him in a manger, because there was no place for them in the inn." When we start singing "Away in the Manger," the words remind us of the words the innkeeper must have told the young couple, the woman being great with child: "There is no room."

Away in a manger
   No crib for His bed
   The little Lord Jesus
   Laid down His sweet head
   The stars in the sky
   Look down where He lay
   The little Lord Jesus
   Asleep on the hay

When we sing "Joy to the World," we make a different choice. Instead of being like the innkeeper and refusing Jesus a room, we make room for Him in our hearts:

Joy to the World , the Lord is come!
  Let earth receive her King;
  Let every heart prepare Him room,
  And Heaven and nature sing,
  And Heaven and nature sing,
  And Heaven, and Heaven, and nature sing.

And the third verse of "O Little Town of Bethlehem" tells us what happens when we make room for Jesus:

How silently, how silently
  The wondrous gift is given
  So God imparts to human hearts
  The blessings of His heaven
  No ear may hear His coming
  But in this world of sin
  Where meek souls will receive him still
  The dear Christ enters in

Don't let the busyness of the season overtake the reason why we sing these Christmas carols. During your Advent journey, take the time to make room for Jesus and allow our dear Christ to enter in!

TODAY'S ACTIVITY: Christmas carols are a sweet tradition during the Advent season. Listen to your favorite ones today and sing along as you reflect on their meaning.

DAY SIXTEEN

In many faith traditions, the focus of the third week of Advent is joy. A quote by S.D. Gordon describes Christian joy:

Joy is distinctly a Christian word and a Christian thing. It is the reverse of happiness. Happiness is the result of what happens of an agreeable sort. Joy has its springs deep down inside. And that spring never runs dry, no matter what happens. Only Jesus gives that joy. He had joy, singing its music within, even under the shadow of the cross.

That is the remarkable thing about joy – it is not a product of our circumstances, but a result of our relationship with Jesus. 1 Peter 1:8-9 reads, "Though you have not seen him, you love him; and even though you do not see him now, you believe in him and are filled with an inexpressible and glorious joy, for you are receiving the end result of your faith, the salvation of your souls." The reason we feel indescribable joy during Advent is because we are anticipating his coming, and we know that in him our salvation is assured!

Paul writes in Philippians 4:4, "Rejoice in the Lord always. I will say it again: Rejoice!" The dictionary defines *rejoice* as to "feel or show great joy." God tells us in His Word to find our joy in Him. When our joy is in the Lord, the things of this world pale in comparison, and we cannot be defeated by the trials of this world. We know from 2 Corinthians 4:18, "For the things that are seen are transient, but the things that are unseen are eternal." How wonderful that we are heirs to eternal salvation and have received everlasting joy, because Jesus was born in a manger on Christmas day!

TODAY'S ACTIVITY: It's easy to get caught up in the tradition of Christmas gift-giving, but remember where your joy comes from: not in any material objects but rather, in your relationship with Jesus. Make a list for Santa that includes ways you can bless others - perhaps request a donation be made to a worthy charity, or ask for a present for a child you know whose family is struggling financially.

DAY SEVENTEEN

As we journey closer to Christmas day and focus on the birth of our Savior, it is good to remember to not only keep Christ in Christmas, but to also invite him into our lives throughout the year. Jesus came down from heaven to save us from our sins. When we call out to him, not only do we receive eternal salvation, we receive his peace on earth. Putting Christ in the center of our lives changes everything. Gaining the eternal perspective of heaven helps us walk in this world with all of its pain and suffering, and enables us to do so with joy. The joy we have in Christ overflows into our relationships and our daily lives, touching others even as it touches us.

As we wait with joyful anticipation for the coming of our King, let us also resolve to keep our focus on him throughout the New Year. Psalm 84:10 tells us, "Better is one day in your courts than a thousand elsewhere;" Let us make every day a day in his courts, and allow the peace of our Savior to permeate our lives, so that it overflows into everything we do.

When our joy is in the Lord, Philippians 4:7 tells us, "And the peace of God, which surpasses all understanding, will guard your hearts and your minds in Christ Jesus." Jesus provides for us what the world can't. Find joy in the baby born on Christmas day, every day, and there you will also find eternal life and the peace that only he can give.

TODAY'S ACTIVITY: Have you been walking with an earthly perspective through your days? Let's pray for God to help you view each day through a heavenly perspective and find joy.

Heavenly Father, I want to experience the abundant life you promised in Scripture. I want to experience joy. It is so easy to get frustrated when things don't go as planned - help me to remember that you have a divine plan that is unfolding and that all I need to do is trust in you and you will make things right, in your timing. Help me view those around me through the same lens that Jesus does - with love and compassion. Help my joy in you overflow and touch the people around me. Amen.

DAY EIGHTEEN

No doubt you have Christmas traditions that you enjoy each year. Many start in our childhoods, and we find comfort and joy in their familiarity. One tradition during Advent for many families, including ours, is that of watching "A Charlie Brown Christmas." The scripture quoted from the second chapter of Luke's Gospel is particularly meaningful. We can have confidence in our Savior because God came down from heaven to save us. Especially powerful are the words "Fear not," referring not just to the fact that a shining angel unexpectedly appeared in the sky, but to all of the fears we carry within us. They are announcing the only one who can rescue us from our fears - the baby in the manger:

And there were in the same country shepherds abiding in the field, keeping watch over their flock by night. And, lo, the angel of the Lord came upon them, and the glory of the Lord shone round about them: and they were sore afraid.

And the angel said unto them, Fear not: [Let this simple command sink in – Don't be afraid of what the future holds, because God holds your future, sealed in the birth of His son] For, behold, I

bring you good tidings of great joy, which shall be to all people. For
unto you is born this day in the city of David a Saviour, which is
Christ the Lord. And this shall be a sign unto you; Ye shall find the
babe wrapped in swaddling clothes, lying in a manger. And
suddenly, there was with the angel a multitude of the heavenly host
praising God, and saying, Glory to God in the highest, and on earth
peace, good will toward men.

The Scriptures Luke 2:8-14 taken from the Holy Bible, King James
Version (1611); in the public domain.

As you continue your Advent journey through the busy and
often chaotic holiday season – remember the true meaning of
Christmas and keep those words from the Gospel of Luke close
to your heart: "Fear not!" [Release your anxieties as you reflect
on these words, and find your security in Jesus instead] "For,
behold, I bring you good tidings of great joy, which shall be to all
people. For unto you is born this day in the city of David a
Saviour, which is Christ the Lord." For that is truly what
Christmas is all about!

TODAY'S ACTIVITY: Make some hot cocoa and pop some
popcorn. Watch "A Charlie Brown Christmas" with family
and/or friends. Take some time afterwards and discuss the parts
you found most meaningful.

"A Charlie Brown Christmas" (1965); Charles M. Schulz,
Produced by Lee Mendelson and Directed by Bill Melendez is
available at a variety of retailers and on Amazon prime.

DAY NINETEEN

John 1:17 tells us, "For the law was given through Moses; grace and truth came through Jesus Christ." Grace is something we are given that we don't deserve. Ephesians 2:8 says, "For by grace you have been saved through faith. And this is not your own doing; it is the gift of God." As we continue our Advent journey, we do so with joy because Jesus brought the richness of God's grace to the world, to save us from our sins. He is our Christmas gift from God!

When I was a teenager in youth group, I remember our youth leader teaching us about grace. He used grace as an acronym and it has stuck with me all these years:

GRACE
   God's
   Riches
   At
   Christ's
   Expense

Our salvation cost Christ everything. It is through his

atoning work at the cross that we experience God's grace – Jesus took our place. Our Savior, Immanuel, "God with us," is also "God in place of us." The miracle of Christmas is that God left the heavens and entered our broken world to save us, instead of allowing us to reap the consequences of our sin. God sent His Son to take our place, so that we can have eternal life with Him. Jesus did it for us because he loves us. We can experience that miracle every day by gratefully living our lives in his grace and truth. Thank you Lord Jesus, for coming to save us! Thank you God, for your gift of grace born on Christmas day!

TODAY'S ACTIVITY: Read Matthew 18:21-35. Walking in God's grace also means extending His grace to others. Is there someone in your life you feel has done you wrong or frustrated you? Make it a point to pray for them today, and ask God to give you the ability to treat them graciously.

DAY TWENTY

As I pondered what to write for today's Advent reflection, the words of an old hymn came to mind:

What a friend we have in Jesus,
All our sins and griefs to bear!
What a privilege to carry
Everything to God in prayer!

It amazes me how the words of this hymn captures the meaning of God's Christmas gift to us in just a few lines. The first line is breathtaking - Jesus is our friend! Jesus teaches us in John 15:13-15, "Greater love has no one than this: to lay down one's life for one's friends. You are my friends if you do what I command. I no longer call you servants, because a servant does not know his master's business. Instead, I have called you friends, for everything that I learned from my Father I have made known to you." How wonderful it is that Jesus calls those who believe in him *friends*! The level of intimacy and affection friends share is available to us with the Son of God!

The second line speaks to God's incredible gift of salvation: it is the hope we have in Jesus because he bore our sins. But he doesn't stop there – not only did he take our place at the cross, he is an ever present comfort when we grieve. He is the friend that we can bring all of our sorrows, disappointments, and heartaches to, and he will carry them for us. He grieves with us and he catches every tear.

The third and fourth lines remind me of the precious gift God gives us – the ability to converse with our friend! We have the incredible blessing of being able to talk to our Savior in prayer. He is not distant, he dwells in our hearts and is available to us every moment of the day.

What a friend we have in Jesus! How wonderful to celebrate his birth, as we look forward to his return. But also how wonderful to know that he is available to us right now as our friend – and he is only a prayer away! Thank you Heavenly Father, for the gift of your Son Jesus, our friend, born on Christmas day!

TODAY'S ACTIVITY: Have you talked to God today? You can talk to Him no matter what you are doing - He is there and listening. Prayer is a great gift from God that allows us to converse with Him about the big things and the little things that we are concerned about. It's an opportunity to tell Him how much we love Him and how grateful we are for what He has done in our lives.

1 Thessalonians 5:16-18 tells us, "Rejoice always, pray continually, give thanks in all circumstances; for this is God's will for you in Christ Jesus." Make it a habit to pray throughout the day - you and your Heavenly Father will be glad that you did!

DAY TWENTY-ONE

Our Advent journey is drawing closer to Christmas day, a day that holds such great significance that we have marked time by it. Our Gregorian calendar is the international standard for designating years based on the traditional estimation of the year Jesus was born. B.C. stands for "Before Christ" and A.D. stands for "Anno Domini," translated from Latin to "In the year of our Lord." How wonderful that the calendar we use more than 2000 years after the birth of Christ signifies his birth as the turning point in world history!

On a personal level, we frequently use Christmas to indicate an event with deep emotional meaning. "Baby's first Christmas" is an oft-used phrase. Couples remember the first Christmas they celebrated together. When we are missing a loved one that is no longer with us, we often struggle with "the first Christmas without them." The birth of Christ is a marker by which we live – it is woven into the tapestry of our lives. Jesus is the Messiah who separates the old and the new! Philippians 2:9-11 says, "Therefore God has highly exalted him and bestowed on him the name that is above every name, so that at the name of Jesus every knee should bow, in heaven and on earth and under the earth, and every tongue confess that Jesus Christ is Lord, to the glory of God the Father." And so, during Advent, we celebrate the coming of our King, who makes all things new. Come Lord Jesus, Come!

TODAY'S ACTIVITY: As you make plans to gather with friends and family, don't forget to include those who may not have a place to go for Christmas. International students are often here without family or friends to spend holidays with. Your neighbor or co-worker may not have a place to go. Invite someone who would otherwise spend Christmas alone to participate in your family's activities. What a lovely way to celebrate our Savior's birth - by sharing the joy you have in His coming with others!

DAY TWENTY-TWO

Christmas time is a time of making special memories. Holiday music playing in the stores, singing Christmas carols at school and church, Christmas concerts, and other festive activities abound. Singing is a wonderful way to express our joy in any season, and singing seems to bring out the excitement and joy that we experience during this special time of Advent. Did you know that the Creator of the universe, the King of kings and Lord of lords, sings over you? Zephaniah 3:17 tells us,

> The Lord your God is in your midst,
>> a mighty one who will save;
>> he will rejoice over you with gladness;
>> he will quiet you by his love;
>> he will exult over you with loud singing.

As you move through the hustle and bustle of holiday preparations, be sure to take some time to be alone in a quiet place and close your eyes. Think about what makes Christmas special to you personally. Thank God for the gift of His son and feel your Heavenly Father's love song washing over you, bringing you the indescribable joy and peace that only He can give.

TODAY'S ACTIVITY: Can you think of a Christmas in the past that was especially meaningful to you? Try to capture the feelings you had and what made it special. Now think about what you can do to make this Christmas special. It does not need to be expensive or elaborate. Sing your favorite Christmas songs. Invite a friend over to make Christmas cookies. Visit a nursing home. Reminisce about past Christmas holidays with family. Take a few minutes to jot down your thoughts and what you plan to do. And if you listen closely, you will hear your Heavenly Father singing over you!

DAY TWENTY-THREE

The faith of Mary, a young woman who trusted God, is remarkable. Although a virgin, when the angel came to her and told her she would conceive and give birth to a son and he would be called the Son of God, her response as recorded in Scripture was "'I am the Lord's servant,' Mary answered. 'May your word to me be fulfilled,'" Luke 1:38. As a result, the world was changed forever. Mary's response is even more extraordinary once you consider the culture in biblical times. To have faith like Mary!

Mary, Did You Know? is a wonderful song composed by Mark Lowry and Buddy Greene, foretelling the great things that Jesus would do. The questions are rhetorical: Mary understood who her son was. The writer uses it as a poignant literary device, and the imagery of the song is an evocative and intimate revelation of Mary's perspective:

When you kiss your little baby, you kiss the face of God.

SCRIPTURE TELLS us in Luke 2:16-19, "So they hurried off and found Mary and Joseph, and the baby, who was lying in the manger. When they had seen him, they spread the word concerning what had been told them about this child, and all who heard it were amazed at what the shepherds said to them. But Mary treasured up all these things and pondered them in her heart." Jesus and his ministry and mission on earth gave his mother much to ponder...

Mary, Did You Know?

MARY DID you know that your baby boy would one day walk on water?
Mary did you know that your baby boy would save our sons and daughters?
Did you know that your baby boy has come to make you new?
This child that you've delivered, will soon deliver you.

MARY DID you know that your baby boy will give sight to a blind man?
Mary did you know that your baby boy will calm a storm with his hand?
Did you know that your baby boy has walked where angels trod?
When you kiss your little baby, you kiss the face of God.

MARY DID YOU KNOW? Mary did you know? Mary did you know?
Mary did you know? Mary did you know? Mary did you know?

The blind will see, the deaf will hear, the dead will live again.
The lame will leap, the dumb will speak, the praises of the lamb.

MARY DID *you know that your baby boy is Lord of all creation?*
Mary did you know that your baby boy would one day rule the nations?
Did you know that your baby boy is heaven's perfect lamb?
The sleeping child you're holding is the great I Am!

MARY DID YOU KNOW? *Mary did you know? Mary did you know?*
Mary did you know? Mary did you know? Mary did you know? Oh,
Mary did you know?

"MARY, DID YOU KNOW?"

～

TODAY'S ACTIVITY: Read Mary's song of praise to the Lord, located in Luke 1:46-55. Mary's hymn is a response to God's mighty work in her life. Take out a piece of paper and write your own hymn of praise to the God who has done great things for you.

DAY TWENTY-FOUR

As I laid in bed this morning, our Advent journey drawing towards the culmination of all of our hopes and preparations, I thought about the capacity I have for fearfulness. I expend way too much time and energy worrying about what might happen. The beautiful thing about our Lord's coming is that we no longer have to be afraid of what the future holds, because he holds our future. It doesn't matter what might happen, because Jesus will be there to carry us through it. The words in the opening verse of "O Little Town of Bethlehem" give voice to the beauty of this truth.

> O little town of Bethlehem, how still we see thee lie!
>> Above thy deep and dreamless sleep the silent stars go by.
>> Yet in thy dark streets shineth the everlasting Light;
>> The hopes and fears of all the years are met in thee tonight.

This quote by artist and blogger Cas Andersen @ la cas de la valise captures the meaning:

O little town of Bethlehem - the whole world has wanted a

reason or a way to meet God without fear - and the whole world will do just that within your small borders. And as Eternity will collide with time and a Son of God is born on earth, so our hopes and fears will collide and neutralize into a little baby... we will realize how accessible He has become... we will realize He is all we need.

Jesus is accessible, and he is all we need. Fear not! Perfect love casts out all fear. Our hope is in him, the everlasting Light! If we would only let ourselves, we can release all of our fears and live in the New Year as God meant us to – no longer afraid but instead, confident in the hope of our Savior born on Christmas day. What an incredible Christmas gift! With grateful hearts, let us allow ourselves to receive it and have a New Year filled with the joy and peace that our Lord came here to give us. Thank you Heavenly Father, for the greatest gift of all! Come Lord Jesus, come!

TODAY'S ACTIVITY: Read the following verses:
Isaiah 43:1
Deuteronomy 31:8
Romans 8:28
Psalm 18:2
John 14:27
Isaiah 41:10

Over and over again God reassures us through His word that we need not fear for He is with us. Choose one of the verses above to memorize, and when you start feeling fearful, focus on God's promises and believe in them. You don't have to be afraid of storms, for you know the One who provides shelter.

CHRISTMAS DAY

Today is the day a tiny baby entered time to save the world. Today humanity escaped death and destruction, finding hope in the birth of a Savior. Today brings meaning to all of our tomorrows. Today provides us with a best friend. I love the words of Carl Medearis, "We know the Creator. We're friends with the King. We know where truth is found. We know what brings life and what gives life and where eternal life resides."

When our son Josh was four years old, I took him to a Christmas Eve service. The church was packed and we were sitting in the middle section. We were listening to the preacher speak when my son decides it's the perfect time to sing Happy Birthday to Jesus. Very loudly. I tried shushing him but he continued, as people turned to look at us. Fortunately, most were smiling and he decided one verse was enough, so the service was able to resume. Josh has been friends with the King from a very young age. The Christmas spirit brings out the child in all of us – may this day of holy birth help us all to have the faith of a child and to be friends with the one true King! Happy Birthday, Lord Jesus!

TODAY'S ACTIVITY: Experience the joy of Christmas through the simple faith of a child. As you move through your day, find time to admire a nativity scene, and in your mind's eye, envision that first Christmas: where in a humble stable, born of a virgin, a baby boy, the Son of God, came to earth to save his people from their sins. Gather everyone around and sing "Happy Birthday" to Jesus. Take joy in knowing that you are friends with the King! He is worthy of our praise, so give him the gift of your gratitude and love, not just today, but each day of the year! Amen!

BENEDICTION

May you continually move away from the mundane, and wake up each morning viewing life through the lens of Advent — finding the miracle of Christmas in each day of the year. Come, Lord Jesus! Come!

POSTSCRIPT

If you enjoyed this devotional, I would love to hear from you. You can email me directly with your comments at nancy@gold-encrossranch.com. I would also appreciate if you could take some time to leave a review on Amazon.

May the grace and peace of our Lord Jesus Christ be with you always,

Nancy Golden

ABOUT THE AUTHOR

Nancy Golden graduated from Dallas Christian College and earned her master's degree from Liberty Baptist Theological Seminary. She is an adjunct faculty member at Dallas Christian College and an instructor for BeADisciple.com

Nancy's seminary work included theology and Bible with an intercultural studies focus. Her passion for evangelism led her to author her first book, *The Second Greatest Commandment Meets the Great Commission: How to Love Your Neighbors to Christ* (HIS Publishing Group, 2013).

Nancy and her husband Phil are active members of the Carrollton Church of the Nazarene in Carrollton, Texas where they serve in various capacities. When she is not busy with her family, students, and church activities, Nancy can be found riding her horse, Pistol, who fortunately does not mind listening to her sing praise and worship songs!

Visit Nancy's blog at https://novelwrites.com/ to learn more about her writing projects and read her ramblings about this journey called life. You can also visit her website http://love2christ.com/ to learn more about how to share your faith and purchase her book on evangelism.

Made in the
USA
Lexington, KY